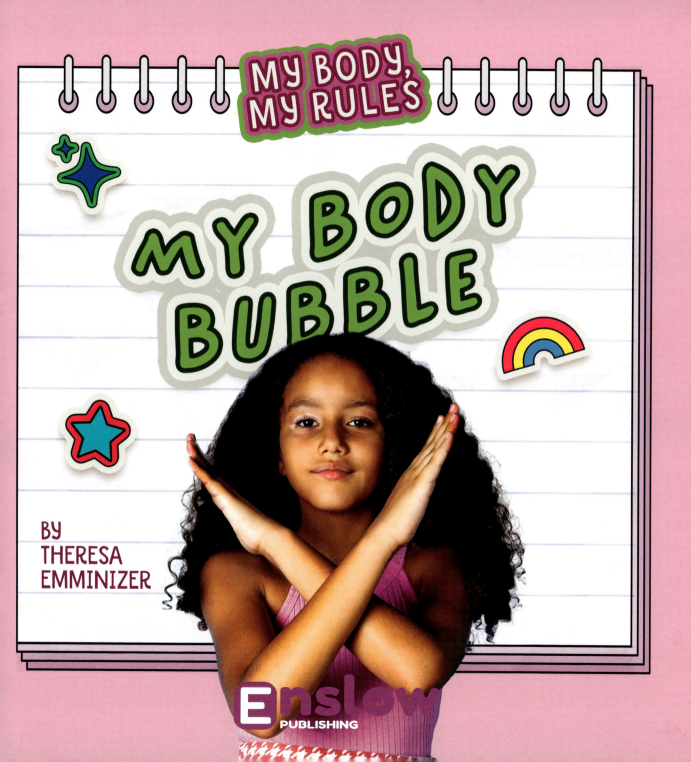

MY BODY, MY RULES

MY BODY BUBBLE

BY THERESA EMMINIZER

Enslow PUBLISHING

Please visit our website, www.enslow.com.
For a free color catalog of all our high-quality books, call toll free 1-800-398-2504 or fax 1-877-980-4454.

Library of Congress Cataloging-in-Publication Data

Names: Emminizer, Theresa, author.
Title: My body bubble / Theresa Emminizer.
Description: [Buffalo] : Enslow Publishing, [2025] | Series: My body, my rules | Includes bibliographical references and index. | Audience: Grades K-1
Identifiers: LCCN 2023053908 (print) | LCCN 2023053909 (ebook) | ISBN 9781978539471 (library binding) | ISBN 9781978539464 (paperback) | ISBN 9781978539488 (ebook)
Subjects: LCSH: Children and strangers–Juvenile literature. | Personal space–Juvenile literature. | Human body–Juvenile literature. | Child sexual abuse–Prevention–Juvenile literature.
Classification: LCC HQ784.S8 E458 2025 (print) | LCC HQ784.S8 (ebook) | DDC 613–dc23/eng/20231201
LC record available at https://lccn.loc.gov/2023053908
LC ebook record available at https://lccn.loc.gov/2023053909

Published in 2025 by
Enslow Publishing
2544 Clinton Street
Buffalo, NY 14224

Copyright © 2025 Enslow Publishing

Designer: Tanya Dellaccio Keeney
Editor: Theresa Emminizer

Photo credits: Series art (notebook) Design PRESENT/Shutterstock.com; series art (stickers) tmn art/Shutterstock.com; cover (girl) Roquillo Tebar/Shutterstock.com; p. 5 Gelpi/Shutterstock.com; pp. 7, 21 fizkes/Shutterstock.com; p. 9 p_ponomareva/Shutterstock.com; p. 11 Ground Picture/Shutterstock.com; p. 13 George Rudy/Shutterstock.com; pp. 15, 19 Prostock-studio/Shutterstock.com; p. 17 Prostock-studio/Shutterstock.com.

All rights reserved.
No part of this book may be reproduced in any form without permission in writing from the publisher, except by a reviewer.

Printed in the United States of America

Some of the images in this book illustrate individuals who are models. The depictions do not imply actual situations or events.

CPSIA compliance information: Batch #CSENS25: For further information contact Enslow Publishing, at 1-800-398-2504.

CONTENTS

YOUR PERSONAL SPACE............4
YOU DECIDE....................6
STOP!.........................8
WHAT TO DO...................10
MY SAFETY CIRCLE.............12
YOUR FEELINGS MATTER.........14
NO SECRETS...................18
YOUR BODY BELONGS TO YOU.....20
WORDS TO KNOW................22
FOR MORE INFORMATION.........23
INDEX........................24

BOLDFACE WORDS APPEAR IN WORDS TO KNOW.

YOUR PERSONAL SPACE

Everybody has a body bubble. This is the **area** of space around your body. Your body belongs only to you! You decide who can come into your body bubble and when. No one should ever touch your body without your **permission**.

YOUR BODY BUBBLE IS SOMETIMES CALLED YOUR PERSONAL SPACE.

YOU DECIDE

You are in charge of your body. You don't ever have to hug or kiss anybody unless you want to. If you don't feel like hugging, say, "No thank you!" You can choose to give a high five, fist bump, or handshake instead.

STOP!

Ani didn't like being tickled. Ani's mom said, "Just tell someone 'No!' if they tickle you." Ani tried. If she was tickled, she said "stop" in a loud, clear voice. But sometimes people didn't listen. They would tickle her anyway!

WHAT TO DO

If someone doesn't stop when you say "no" or "stop," tell a safe adult right away. A safe adult will always listen to you and help you. They won't make you feel bad. If that safe adult doesn't help, tell another safe adult.

MY SAFETY CIRCLE

Cohen has a safety circle. These are five grown-ups he can trust. Cohen's safety circle is his mom, dad, uncle, grandma, and teacher. Cohen can tell them anything. He knows they'll always listen to him and help keep him safe.

AT LEAST ONE PERSON IN YOUR SAFETY CIRCLE SHOULD BE A NONFAMILY MEMBER.

YOUR FEELINGS MATTER

It can be hard to say "no" when someone touches you and you don't want to be touched. It's especially hard when you are speaking to a friend, teacher, or family member. You might be scared of hurting their feelings. But your feelings are just as important!

Feelings can be **confusing**, especially those about your body. Hugs might feel great when they come from your mom, but not from another person. Who comes into your body bubble is your decision! You don't have to explain why you are saying "no."

OTHER PEOPLE SHOULD RESPECT YOUR BODY BUBBLE.

NO SECRETS

If someone tells you to keep a secret and it makes you feel uncomfortable, don't listen. Tell a grown-up in your safety circle right away. You won't get into trouble. Don't worry about getting anyone else into trouble, either. Your safety and feelings are more important than anything else.

YOUR BODY BELONGS TO YOU

You are the boss of your body. You don't have to touch anyone or let them touch you unless you feel like it. Even if somebody hugs you once, you can say "no" next time. Listen to your feelings and use your voice!

YOUR BODY, YOUR RULES!

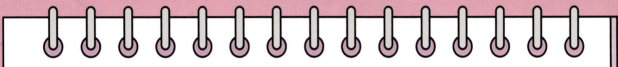

area: The space around something or someone.

confusing: Hard to understand.

permission: Saying something is OK or allowing something to happen.

uncomfortable: Feeling unhappy or unsure about something.

FOR MORE INFORMATION

BOOKS

McAneney, Caitie. *I Talk to Cope*. New York, NY: PowerKids Press, 2023.

Ridley, Sarah. *Being Safe*. New York, NY: PowerKids Press, 2023.

WEBSITES

Kids Health: Talk About Your Feelings
kidshealth.org/en/kids/talk-feelings.html
Learn about how to talk about your feelings.

Kids Health: Abuse: What Kids Need to Know
kidshealth.org/en/kids/handle-abuse.html
Learn what to do if someone is harming you.

Publisher's note to educators and parents: Our editors have carefully reviewed these websites to ensure that they are suitable for students. Many websites change frequently, however, and we cannot guarantee that a site's future contents will continue to meet our high standards of quality and educational value. Be advised that students should be closely supervised whenever they access the internet.

Index

body bubble, 4, 5, 16, 17
family, 9, 13, 14
feelings, 14, 18
feeling uncomfortable, 15, 16
fist bump, 6
handshake, 6
high five, 6
hugs, 6, 16, 20
kisses, 6

permission, 4
personal space, 5
safety circle, 10, 12, 13, 18
saying "no," 6, 7, 8, 9, 10, 14, 20
scared, 14
secrets, 17, 18, 19
tickling, 8
using your voice, 20